AFFILIATE MARKETING SIMPLIFIED

"Demystifying Profit: The
Ultimate Guide to Simplified
Affiliate Marketing"

VINCENT SIMS

Dedication

"To those who dare to dream of financial freedom through digital pathways, this book is dedicated to your journey. May 'Affiliate Marketing Simplified' be your compass in navigating the realm of online prosperity."

Table of Contents

Acknowledgments

"I extend my deepest gratitude to all the mentors, industry experts, and tireless trailblazers who generously shared their wisdom. This book stands as a collective effort, and I am immensely thankful for the invaluable insights that have shaped 'Affiliate Marketing Simplified.' Special thanks to my family and everybody for your unwavering support on this enlightening journey."

Preface

"In an era where digital opportunities abound, 'Affiliate Marketing Simplified' emerges as a guide through the intricate landscape of online commerce. This preface marks the beginning of a journey aimed at demystifying the world of affiliate marketing, distilling complex strategies into accessible knowledge. As we embark on this exploration together, let the simplicity of these insights be the catalyst for your success in the dynamic realm of affiliate marketing."

Foreword

"As the digital horizon expands, 'Affiliate Marketing Simplified' emerges as a beacon of clarity in the intricate realm of online entrepreneurship. In this foreword, we set sail into the ever-evolving world of affiliate marketing—a landscape of opportunity and innovation. With a commitment to simplicity, this book charts a course through strategies, insights, and practical wisdom, inviting both novices and seasoned marketers to embark on a journey of growth and prosperity. May this guide empower you to navigate the currents of affiliate marketing with confidence and ease."

Chapter 1

Introduction to Affiliate Marketing

- Understanding the Basics

Affiliate marketing serves as a dynamic avenue for individuals and businesses alike to capitalize on the vast landscape of online commerce. At its core, the concept revolves around a symbiotic relationship between three key players: the advertiser, the affiliate, and the consumer.

1. Advertiser:

- Advertisers, also known as merchants or vendors, are the creators or sellers of a product or service.

- They leverage affiliate marketing to expand their reach by partnering with individuals or entities willing to promote their offerings.

2 - Affiliates, often content creators, bloggers, or influencers, act as intermediaries between advertisers and consumers.

- By joining affiliate programs, they gain access to unique tracking links or promotional materials to share with their audience.

- Affiliates earn commissions for every sale, click, or lead generated through their unique affiliate link.

3. Consumer:

- The end consumer is the ultimate target of affiliate marketing efforts.

- They discover products or services through affiliate-promoted content and, when making a purchase or taking a desired action, contribute to the affiliate's commission.

Key Components of Affiliate Marketing:

1. Affiliate Networks:

- Many affiliates join networks that connect them with a multitude of advertisers.

- These networks simplify the process by providing a centralized platform for affiliates to discover and join various affiliate programs.

2. Tracking and Analytics:

- Precise tracking is fundamental to affiliate marketing success. Unique affiliate links, cookies, and tracking pixels help monitor user interactions and attribute conversions to the correct affiliate.

3. Commission Structures:

- Commissions vary and can be based on different models such as Pay-Per-Sale (PPS), Pay-Per-Click (PPC), or Pay-Per-Lead (PPL).

- Understanding the commission structure is crucial for affiliates to assess the potential earnings from promoting a particular product or service.

4. Content and Trust:

- Successful affiliates focus on creating high-quality, relevant content that resonates with their audience.

- Building trust is paramount. Audiences are more likely to make a purchase based on recommendations from sources they trust.

5. Compliance and Ethics:
    - Adhering to ethical practices and legal guidelines is essential in affiliate marketing.
    - Disclosures and transparency regarding affiliate relationships help maintain trust with the audience.

Affiliate marketing, in its simplified essence, revolves around forging mutually beneficial connections. Advertisers gain exposure, affiliates earn commissions, and consumers discover valuable products or services. As you delve into the basics of affiliate marketing, remember that authenticity, transparency, and a genuine understanding of your audience are the cornerstones of a successful affiliate journey.

- Evolution of Affiliate Marketing

The evolution of affiliate marketing is a fascinating journey that mirrors the dynamic shifts in the digital landscape. From its humble beginnings, affiliate marketing has transformed into a sophisticated and integral component of online commerce.

1. Emergence in the 1990s:
    - The concept of affiliate marketing took root in the mid-1990s, primarily with the idea of revenue sharing.
    - Amazon is often credited with launching one of the earliest affiliate programs in 1996, allowing website owners to earn commissions by promoting Amazon products.

2. Early Challenges and Innovations:
    - In its early days, affiliate marketing faced skepticism and

challenges related to tracking and attribution.

- Innovations in tracking technologies, such as cookies, played a pivotal role in addressing these challenges and establishing more reliable affiliate systems.

3. Rise of Affiliate Networks:

- The late 1990s and early 2000s saw the rise of affiliate networks, acting as intermediaries between advertisers and affiliates.

- These networks streamlined the affiliate marketing process by providing a centralized platform for managing programs and tracking performance.

4. Expansion of E-commerce:

- The boom of e-commerce in the 2000s contributed significantly to the growth of affiliate marketing.

- Retailers and businesses increasingly recognized the value of leveraging affiliates to drive traffic and sales.

5. Shift to Performance Marketing:

- Affiliate marketing evolved into a form of performance marketing, where advertisers pay affiliates based on measurable results like sales, clicks, or leads.

- This shift made affiliate marketing more accountable and ROI-focused.

6.   Influencer   Marketing Integration:
    - With the rise of social media and influencer culture, affiliate marketing is seamlessly integrated with influencer marketing.
    - Content creators, bloggers, and social media influencers became prominent affiliates, leveraging their audiences to promote products and earn commissions.

7. Technological Advancements:
    - Technological advancements, including sophisticated tracking

tools, data analytics, and automation, have further refined affiliate marketing strategies.

- Artificial intelligence and machine learning have been increasingly used to optimize targeting and improve conversion rates.

8. Globalization and Diversification:

- Affiliate marketing has become a global phenomenon, transcending geographical boundaries.

- Diversification in niche markets and the inclusion of various industries beyond e-commerce, such as finance, travel, and software, showcase the versatility of affiliate marketing.

9. Regulatory Compliance:

- As the industry matured, there has been a greater emphasis on regulatory compliance and ethical practices.

- Adherence to guidelines and transparency in affiliate relationships have become crucial for maintaining trust.

10. Future Trends:

- Looking ahead, the future of affiliate marketing is likely to be shaped by emerging technologies, increased personalization, and a continued emphasis on building authentic connections with audiences.

In summary, the evolution of affiliate marketing has been marked by innovation, adaptability, and a relentless pursuit of efficiency. From its early days as a revenue-sharing experiment to its current status as a sophisticated performance marketing channel, affiliate marketing continues to thrive in the ever-evolving digital ecosystem.

Chapter 2

Choosing Profitable Niches

- Market Research Strategies

Market research is a crucial component of strategic business planning, providing valuable insights that can shape decisions and drive success. Effective market research strategies involve a systematic approach to collecting, analyzing, and interpreting information about a target market. Here are key strategies to conduct comprehensive market research:

1. Define Objectives and Scope:
   - Clearly articulate the goals of your market research. Understand what specific information you seek and define the scope of your study.
   - Determine whether you're exploring a new market, evaluating customer preferences, or assessing competition.

2. Identify Target Audience:
   - Define the demographic, geographic, and psychographic characteristics of your target audience.

- Tailor your research methods to effectively reach and gather insights from your specific audience segments.

3. Choose Research Methods:
- Utilize a mix of quantitative and qualitative research methods. Surveys, interviews, focus groups, and observations are common techniques.
- Online surveys, social media listening, and data analytics tools can provide quantitative insights, while interviews and focus groups offer qualitative depth.

4. Analyze Competitors:

- Assess the competitive landscape by identifying key competitors and analyzing their strengths, weaknesses, opportunities, and threats (SWOT analysis).

- Understand market gaps and areas where your product or service can offer a unique value proposition.

5. Stay Updated on Industry Trends:

- Monitor industry trends, technological advancements, and regulatory changes that might impact your market.

- Subscribe to industry publications, attend conferences,

and engage in continuous learning to stay informed.

6. Leverage Secondary Data:
- Gather information from existing sources, such as industry reports, government publications, and academic studies.
- Secondary data provides a foundation for understanding market trends and can complement primary research efforts.

7. Conduct SWOT Analysis:
- Perform a comprehensive SWOT analysis to identify internal strengths and weaknesses as well

as external opportunities and threats.

- This analysis helps in developing strategies that capitalize on strengths and address weaknesses.

8. Focus on Customer Feedback:
- Actively seek and analyze customer feedback through surveys, reviews, and direct interactions.
- Understand customer needs, preferences, and pain points to refine your products or services.

9. Consider Cultural and Ethical Factors:

- Be mindful of cultural nuances and ethical considerations, especially in global markets.

- Cultural understanding is crucial for successful market penetration and maintaining a positive brand image.

10. Test and Iterate:

- Pilot test new products, services, or marketing strategies in a controlled environment.

- Use feedback from pilot tests to iterate and refine your offerings before a full-scale launch.

11. Embrace Technology:

- Leverage technology tools for data collection, analysis, and visualization.

- Artificial intelligence and machine learning can provide advanced insights and predictions based on large datasets.

12. Budget and Timeline Planning:
- Develop a realistic budget and timeline for your market research initiatives.

- Balancing thoroughness with efficiency is key to obtaining valuable insights within constraints.

By adopting a comprehensive market research strategy,

businesses can uncover hidden opportunities, mitigate risks, and make informed decisions that contribute to sustainable growth in today's competitive landscape.

- Identifying High-Converting Niches

Identifying high-converting niches is a pivotal step in developing a successful business strategy. A niche market represents a segment of the market that has unique needs or preferences, and focusing on such niches can lead to higher conversion rates. Here are effective ways to identify high-converting niches:

1. Analyze Your Interests and Expertise:
   - Begin by evaluating your interests, skills, and expertise. Identifying a niche aligned with your passion can enhance your commitment and understanding of the market.

2. Conduct Market Research:
   - Use comprehensive market research to understand current trends, customer behaviors, and emerging opportunities.

- Analyze competitor landscapes to identify gaps or underserved segments within the market.

3. Explore Sub-Niches:
    - Dive deeper into broader niches by exploring sub-niches. These smaller segments may have specific needs that are not fully addressed by mainstream products or services.

4. Evaluate Demand and Competition:
    - Gauge the demand for products or services within potential niches. Tools like keyword research, Google Trends, and industry reports can provide insights.

- Assess the level of competition in each niche to identify areas with less saturation and more opportunities for differentiation.

5. Consider Evergreen Niches:
   - Explore evergreen niches that have consistent demand over time. Industries such as health, personal finance, and self-improvement often maintain stable interests.

6. Analyze Consumer Pain Points:
   - Identify common challenges or pain points experienced by consumers. Creating solutions that a

7. Leverageddress these issues can lead to high-converting niches.

Trends and Emerging Markets:

- Keep an eye on emerging trends and markets. Early entry into a growing niche can establish your brand as a leader and capture a significant market share.

8. Evaluate Profitability:

- Consider the profitability of potential niches. Assess the willingness of consumers in the niche to spend money on products or services.

- High-value niches often involve consumers who are more willing to invest in solutions that meet their specific needs.

9. Understand Target Audience Behavior:

- Gain a deep understanding of the behaviors, preferences, and buying patterns of your target audience within each niche.

- Tailor marketing strategies and product offerings to align with the unique characteristics of your chosen niche.

10. Test and Iterate:

- Conduct small-scale tests or pilot projects within identified niches to gauge actual conversion rates.

- Use feedback and performance metrics to refine your approach and offerings iteratively.

11. Stay Flexible and Adaptive:
- Markets evolve, and consumer preferences change. Stay flexible and adaptive to shifts in the landscape, allowing your business to pivot when necessary.

12. Seek Feedback from Your Audience:
- Engage with your audience through surveys, social media, or direct communication. Gather insights on their preferences and pain points to fine-tune your niche strategy.

Identifying high-converting niches requires a combination of research, intuition, and adaptability. By aligning your business with niche markets that have genuine demand and addressing specific customer needs, you can position yourself for sustained success in a competitive business environment.

Chapter 3

Building a Solid Affiliate Website

- Creating a User-Friendly Design

Creating a user-friendly design is paramount for engaging and satisfying online visitors. A user-friendly website or application enhances the overall user experience, encourages longer interactions, and promotes repeat visits. Here are key principles to consider when crafting a user-friendly design:

1. Intuitive Navigation:

- Prioritize intuitive navigation that allows users to easily find the information they seek.

- Implement clear menu structures, logical page hierarchies, and straightforward navigation paths.

2. Responsive Design:

- Ensure your design is responsive and adapts seamlessly to various devices and screen sizes.

- Mobile-friendly layouts are essential for catering to the increasing number of users accessing websites through smartphones and tablets.

3. Consistent Branding and Design Elements:
- Maintain consistency in branding elements such as color schemes, fonts, and logos throughout the website or application.
- Consistency fosters a sense of familiarity and professionalism, contributing to a cohesive user experience.

4. Clear and Concise Content:
- Present content clearly and concisely, avoiding unnecessary jargon or clutter.

- Use readable fonts, appropriate spacing, and well-organized layouts to enhance content readability.

5. Minimized Load Times:
- Optimize images, code, and other elements to minimize page load times.
- Fast-loading pages improve user satisfaction and contribute to better search engine rankings.

6. User-Centric Forms:
- Design forms with the user in mind, minimizing the number of required fields and providing helpful error messages.

- Use logical input fields and consider implementing features like autofill to streamline the form-filling process.

7. Accessibility Considerations:
- Ensure your design is accessible to users with disabilities. Follow accessibility guidelines, such as providing alternative text for images and ensuring keyboard navigation is functional.

8. Call-to-Action Clarity:
- Highlight call-to-action buttons and make them easily distinguishable.

- Use persuasive language to guide users toward desired actions, such as making a purchase or signing up for a newsletter.

9. Visual Hierarchy:

- Establish a visual hierarchy to guide users through the most important elements on a page.

- Prioritize content based on importance, using font size, color, and spacing to create a clear visual flow.

10. User Feedback and Error Handling:

- Provide feedback to users after actions, such as successful form submissions or error messages.

- Communicate errors and offer guidance on how users can rectify the situation.

11. User Testing:

- Conduct user testing to gather feedback on the usability of your design.

- Analyze user behavior and make iterative improvements based on observed patterns and user suggestions.

12. Mobile-Friendly Touch Targets:

- Ensure that interactive elements, such as buttons and links, are touch-friendly on mobile devices.

- Optimal touch target sizes and spacing prevent user frustration and improve overall usability.

A user-friendly design is an ongoing process that involves continuous refinement based on user feedback and evolving best practices. By prioritizing ease of use, clear communication, and a seamless overall experience, you can create a design that resonates positively with your audience.

- Optimizing for SEO and Conversions

To optimize for both SEO (Search Engine Optimization) and conversions, it's essential to strike a balance between catering to search engines and providing a user-friendly experience. Here are key strategies to achieve this synergy:

1. Keyword Research:
   - Identify relevant keywords that align with your content and target audience.
   - Focus on long-tail keywords to capture specific search queries.

2. Quality Content:

- Create high-quality, valuable content that addresses user intent.

- Use a natural language that resonates with your audience while incorporating targeted keywords.

3. Mobile Optimization:

- Ensure your website is mobile-friendly, as mobile optimization is a crucial SEO factor.

- A responsive design enhances user experience, positively impacting conversion rates.

4. Page Speed:

- Optimize your website for quick loading times. Slow pages can deter users and affect search rankings.
- Compress images, leverage browser caching, and minimize HTTP requests.

5. User-Friendly Navigation:
- Design an intuitive website structure for easy navigation.
- Clear calls-to-action (CTAs) guide users through the conversion funnel.

6. Meta Tags:
- Craft compelling meta titles and descriptions with relevant keywords.

- Meta tags serve as a preview in search results and can influence click-through rates.

7. Optimized Images:
- Use descriptive file names and alt text for images to enhance accessibility and SEO.
- Compressed images contribute to faster page loading.

8. Internal Linking:
- Implement strategic internal linking to guide users to relevant content within your site.
- This aids in SEO and keeps visitors engaged, potentially leading to conversions.

9. Social Media Integration:

- Leverage social media platforms to promote your content and engage with your audience.

- Social signals can indirectly impact SEO, and social media serves as an additional conversion channel.

10. Responsive Design:

- Ensure a seamless user experience across various devices and screen sizes.

- Responsive design contributes to better rankings and improved conversion rates.

11. A/B Testing:

- Continuously test different elements of your website, such as headlines, CTAs, and layouts.
- Data-driven insights from A/B testing help refine your site for optimal conversion rates.

12. Analytics: - Use analytics tools to monitor user behavior, track conversions, and identify areas for improvement.
- Data-driven decisions can lead to ongoing enhancements in both SEO and conversion optimization.

By integrating these strategies, you can create a website that not only ranks well in search engines but also converts visitors into customers effectively. Regularly update your approach based on evolving SEO trends and user preferences to stay ahead in the digital landscape.

Chapter 4.

Effective Affiliate Strategies

- Content Marketing Techniques

Content marketing is a powerful strategy that involves creating and distributing valuable, relevant content to attract and engage a target audience. Here are some effective content marketing techniques to enhance your online presence and drive results:

1. Define Your Audience:

- Identify your target audience to tailor content that resonates with their needs, preferences, and pain points.

2. Content Calendar:

- Develop a content calendar to plan and organize your content creation efforts. Consistency is key for audience engagement.

3. Educational Content:

- Share informative and educational content that adds value to your audience's knowledge. How-to guides, tutorials, and insights can establish your brand as an authority in your industry.

4. Storytelling:
- Craft compelling narratives that connect emotionally with your audience. Stories create a memorable and relatable brand identity.

5. Visual Content:
- Incorporate visually appealing elements such as infographics, videos, and images to enhance the

user experience. Visual content is often more shareable and engaging.

6. SEO Optimization:

- Integrate relevant keywords naturally into your content to improve search engine visibility. SEO-friendly content can attract organic traffic.

7. Social Media Integration:

- Share your content across various social media platforms to broaden your reach. Tailor your content for each platform to maximize engagement.

8. Email Marketing:

- Utilize email campaigns to distribute content directly to your audience. Newsletters, updates, and exclusive content can foster a deeper connection.

9. Interactive Content:
- Create interactive content like quizzes, polls, or surveys to boost engagement. Interactive elements encourage participation and capture valuable data.

10. User-Generated Content:
- Encourage your audience to create and share content related to your brand. User-generated content builds community and authenticity.

11. Influencer Collaborations:

- Partner with influencers in your industry to amplify your content. Influencers can bring a new audience and credibility to your brand.

12. Content Upcycling:

- Repurpose existing content into different formats. For example, turn a blog post into a podcast episode or an infographic. This extends the life and reaches of your content.

13. Content Distribution:

- Leverage various distribution channels, including guest posting, partnerships, and syndication. Reach your audience where they are already active online.

14. Analytics and Optimization:
     - Regularly analyze content performance using analytics tools. Adjust your strategy based on what works best for your audience.

15. Evergreen Content:
     - Create timeless, evergreen content that remains relevant over an extended period. This type of content continues to attract traffic and engagement.

16. Podcasting:

- Enter the podcasting space to connect with audiences through audio content. Podcasts offer a convenient and on-the-go way for users to an effective strategy that not only attracts your target audience but also fosters long-term relationships and consumes information.

By implementing these content marketing techniques, you can build robust and, brand loyalty, and business growth.

- Social Media and Email Marketing

Implementing effective affiliate strategies, particularly through social media and email marketing, can significantly boost your affiliate program's success. Here's a guide on leveraging these channels for optimal results:

Affiliate Strategies: Social Media

1. Identify the Right Platforms:

- Focus on social media platforms where your target audience is most active. Each platform has its unique dynamics, so tailor your approach accordingly.

2. Engage Influencers:
- Collaborate with social media influencers who align with your brand. Influencers can effectively promote your affiliate products to their engaged audience.

3. Create Compelling Visuals:
- Visual content tends to perform well on social media. Craft eye-catching graphics, videos, and infographics to

showcase your affiliate products appealingly.

4. Use Hashtags Strategically:

- Implement relevant and trending hashtags to increase the discoverability of your affiliate posts. Research and choose hashtags that resonate with your target audience.

5. Run Contests and Giveaways:

- Encourage engagement by organizing contests or giveaways tied to your affiliate products. This not only increases brand visibility but also attracts potential customers.

6. Share Authentic Stories:

- Humanize your brand by sharing authentic stories related to your affiliate products. User testimonials and personal experiences can build trust and credibility.

7. Leverage Social Ads:

- Boost your affiliate content through targeted social media advertising. Utilize the ad platforms to reach specific demographics and expand your affiliate reach.

8. Track and Analyze Performance:

- Use analytics tools to monitor the performance of your affiliate campaigns on social media. Analyze data to understand what resonates with your audience and refine your strategy accordingly.

Affiliate Strategies: Email Marketing

1. Build a Quality Email List:
   - Prioritize building a targeted and engaged email list. Segment your list based on user preferences and behaviors for personalized communication.

2. Craft Compelling Emails:

- Write persuasive and concise emails that communicate the value of the affiliate products. Use compelling subject lines to increase open rates.

3. Provide Exclusive Offers:
   - Offer exclusive discounts or promotions to your email subscribers. This creates a sense of exclusivity and encourages conversions.

4. Implement Drip Campaigns:- Set up automated drip campaigns to nurture leads over time. Gradually introduce your affiliate products and highlight their

benefits through a series of emails.

5. Use Visuals in Emails:
- Incorporate visually appealing elements in your email campaigns. Include product images, GIFs, or videos to showcase the affiliate products effectively.

6. Optimize for Mobile:
- Ensure that your emails are mobile-friendly. A significant portion of users access emails on mobile devices, and an optimized layout enhances the user experience.

7.   Segmentation   and Personalization:

- Utilize segmentation and personalization strategies to tailor your emails to specific audience segments. Personalized content increases   engagement   and conversion rates.

8. Include Clear CTAs

- Clearly state the call-to-action (CTA) in your emails. Whether it's making a purchase or visiting a landing page, a well-defined CTA guides   subscribers   toward conversion.

9. Monitor Email Metrics:

- Track key email metrics such as open rates, click-through rates, and conversion rates. Use this data to refine your email strategy and optimize future campaigns.

By integrating these strategies into your affiliate marketing efforts, you can harness the power of social media and email marketing ē maximize reach, engagement, and ultimately, conversions for your affiliate products. Regularly assess performance and adapt your approach based on insights gained from analytics.

Chapter 5.

Maximizing Earnings and Scaling

- Advanced Affiliate Tactics

In the dynamic landscape of affiliate marketing, staying ahead requires a strategic approach that goes beyond the basics. Here are some advanced affiliate tactics to elevate your game:

1. Data-Driven Decision Making:
    Leverage analytics tools to analyze user behavior, track

conversions, and identify high-performing channels. Use this data to refine your strategies and focus on what works.

2. Segmentation and Personalization:

Tailor your campaigns based on audience segments. Implement personalized content, offers, and communication to engage users on a more individual level, increasing the likelihood of conversion.

3. Multi-Channel Marketing:

Diversify your presence across various platforms such as social media, email, and content marketing. A multi-channel approach broadens your reach and helps you connect with diverse audiences.

4. Advanced SEO Techniques:
Master advanced SEO strategies to optimize your content for search engines. This includes on-page SEO, backlink building, and staying updated with algorithm changes to maintain high visibility.

5. Cross-Device Tracking:
Implement cross-device tracking to understand the user journey seamlessly across different platforms. This enables a more

comprehensive view of your audience and their interactions with your affiliate links.

6. Conversion Rate Optimization (CRO):

Focus on refining the user experience to boost conversion rates. A/B testing, heatmaps, and user feedback can help identify areas for improvement and enhance the overall effectiveness of your campaigns.

7. Advanced Copywriting Techniques:

Hone your copywriting skills to craft compelling and persuasive content. Understand the psychology of persuasion and employ storytelling techniques to create a strong emotional connection with your audience.

8. Deep Linking Strategies:

Instead of directing traffic to the homepage, use deep linking to direct users to specific product pages. This enhances user experience, increases relevance, and can lead to higher conversion rates.

9. Partnership and Collaboration:

Forge strategic partnerships with influencers, bloggers, or other affiliates. Collaborative efforts can amplify your reach and lend credibility to your promotions.

10. Dynamic Retargeting:
Implement dynamic retargeting campaigns to re-engage users who have previously interacted with your content. Show them personalized ads featuring products or services they've shown interest in.

By incorporating these advanced affiliate tactics into your marketing arsenal, you'll not only stay competitive but also open up new avenues for success in the ever-evolving affiliate landscape.

- Scaling Your Affiliate Business for Long-Term Success

Achieving long-term success in the affiliate marketing realm requires a strategic and scalable approach. Here's a comprehensive guide on how to scale your affiliate business for sustained growth:

1. Build a Strong Foundation:
   Lay the groundwork with a solid niche selection and robust website. Ensure your platform is user-friendly, optimized for search engines, and provides a seamless experience for visitors.

2. Diversify Your Offerings:

Expand your product or service range within your niche. Diversification not only attracts a broader audience but also safeguards your business against fluctuations in market trends.

3. Automation and Efficiency:

Implement automation tools to streamline repetitive tasks. This includes email marketing, social media scheduling, and data analysis. Efficiency gains allow you to focus on strategic aspects of your business.

4. Invest in Quality Content:

Content remains king. Invest in high-quality, evergreen content that not only attracts visitors but also establishes your authority within the niche. This content becomes a valuable asset for long-term SEO benefits.

5. Scale Your Advertising Efforts: Gradually increase your advertising budget across effective channels. Utilize paid search, social media ads, and other platforms strategically to reach a wider audience and drive targeted traffic.

6. Optimize Conversion Funnel:

Continuously optimize your conversion funnel. Analyze user behavior, conduct A/B testing, and refine your landing pages to enhance the user experience and maximize conversion rates.

7. Global Expansion:

Explore opportunities to go global. Identify markets where your niche has untapped potential and tailor your strategies to accommodate international audiences, including localization of content and advertising.

8. Affiliate Recruitment and Management:

Build a network of affiliates to promote your products or services. Efficiently manage relationships by offering competitive commissions, providing promotional materials, and fostering open communication.

9. Customer Retention Strategies:
Prioritize customer retention as much as acquisition. Implement loyalty programs, engage with your audience through newsletters and social media, and offer exclusive deals to encourage repeat business.

10. Continuous Learning and Adaptation:

Stay informed about industry trends and technological advancements. Embrace a mindset of continuous learning and be ready to adapt your strategies to stay ahead in the ever-evolving affiliate marketing landscape.

11. Monitor Key Performance (KPIs):

Regularly assess your KPIs to gauge the effectiveness of your strategies. Track metrics like conversion rates, customer lifetime value, and return on investment to make informed decisions for future scaling.

By implementing these strategies and maintaining a focus on sustainability and adaptability, you position your affiliate business for not just short-term gains but enduring success in the competitive affiliate marketing ecosystem.